STARRY
MESSENGER

A book depicting the life of a
famous scientist · mathematician
astronomer · philosopher
physicist

GALILEO GALILEI

Created and illustrated by
PETER SÍS

for

FRANCES FOSTER BOOKS

at

FARRAR · STRAUS · GIROUX
NEW YORK

For Frances

Copyright © 1996 by Peter Sís
All rights reserved
Distributed in Canada by Douglas & McIntyre Ltd.
Color separations by Hong Kong Scanner Arts
First edition, 1996
Sunburst edition, 2000
Printed in May 2009 in China by Kwong Fat Offset Printing,
Dao Jiao District, Dongguan City
7 9 10 8

Library of Congress Cataloging-in-Publication Data
Sís, Peter
Starry Messenger : a book depicting the life of a famous
scientist, mathematician, astronomer, philosopher, physicist,
Galileo Galilei / created and illustrated by Peter Sís.
p. cm.
ISBN 978-0-374-47027-2
1. Galilei, Galileo 1564-1642—Biography—Juvenile literature.
2. Astronomers—Italy—Biography—Juvenile literature.
3. Scientists—Italy—Biography—Juvenile literature. [1. Galielo,
1564-1642. 2. Scientisits.] I. Title.
QB36.G2S57 1996 520'.92-dc20 [B] 95-44986

Galileo Galilei's words quoted from *Discoveries and Opinions of Galileo*,
translated by Stillman Drake. Copyright © 1957 by Stillman Drake.
Used by permission of Doubleday, a division of Bantam Doubleday Dell Publishing Group, Inc.

With thanks to Professors Peter Galison and Mario Biagioli, both of Harvard University,
for their critical help in the making of this book.

THE
PTOLEMAIC
SYSTEM

THE
EARTH
STANDS STILL

EUDOXUS
(408-355 B.C.)

ARISTOTLE
(384-322 B.C.)

PTOLEMY
(A.D. 150)

"God fixed the Earth upon its foundation, not to be moved for ever." ... PSALMS

For hundreds of years, most people thought the earth was the center of the universe, and the sun and the moon and all the other planets revolved around it. They did not doubt or wonder if this was true. They just followed tradition.

THE
COPERNICAN
SYSTEM

Then one man looked at the sky and wondered: "What if things are not as everybody believes them to be? Maybe the earth and the other planets move around the sun." He wrote down his observations, but he did not talk about them, and he did not publish them for a long, long time. He knew he could not prove they were true. It would take someone else to do that . . .

THE
EARTH
MOVES!

Italy was a quilt of city-states, each with its own laws and government. A common religion, the Catholic Faith, was one thing they all shared, and the Church was a powerful influence.

In those days, Italy was a country where many great artists, writers, musicians, and scholars lived.

Papal States

Duchy Of Tuscany

Republic Of Genoa

Roman Empire

Kingdom Of France

Duchy Of Modena

Duchy Of Savoy

GALILEO'S ITALY

Kingdom Of Naples

Republic Of Venice

Duchy Of Milan

Ottoman Empire

Duchy Of Ferrara

Marquisate Of Montferrat

VENICE

PADUA

FLORENCE

ROME

Kingdom Of Sardinia

Republic Of Lucca

Kingdom Of Sicily

Marquisate Of Mantova

*Galileo Galilei
born February 15, 1564*

*Father: Vincenzio Galilei, cloth merchant,
accomplished musician, and mathematician.*

*William Shakespeare was also born in 1564.
Michelangelo died in that same year.*

"Be not afraid of greatness: some are born great, some achieve greatness, and some have greatness thrust upon them." —William Shakespeare, *Twelfth Night* (II.v.157)

In the city of Pisa, a little boy was born with stars in his eyes. His parents named him Galileo.

Until the age of eleven, Galileo was taught at home by his father. Then he was sent to the Benedictine Monastery of Santa Maria di Vallombrosa where he studied Latin, Greek, religion and music.

In Galileo's time, homes and cities were often lit from candles or oil lamps. There was no refrigeration. This is the reason that thousands died from typhus and from the bubonic plague. Life was difficult and luxuries few. Light came from candles or oil lamps. Disease was common, and

Galileo thrived and he grew. In many ways he was like any other healthy child, but he was more curious than most and stars were always on his mind.

1581

Entered the University of Pisa. Was an argumentative student and questioned the teachings of Aristotle. Left the university to study mathematics and physics on his own. Became Professor of Mathematics at the University of Pisa when he was just twenty-five years old.

1592. Became Professor of Mathematics at the University of Padua.

Did experiments proving Aristotle wrong. Discovered the Law of Falling Objects by showing that two balls of unequal weight fall at the same speed.

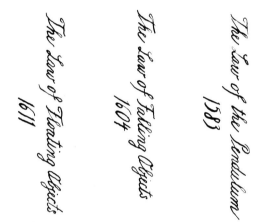

The Law of the Pendulum 1583

The Law of Falling Objects 1604

The Law of Floating Objects 1611

Invented and perfected instruments that brought new accuracy to science: a hydrostatic balance, the first practical thermometer, a geometric and military compass, a compound microscope, and the first astronomical telescope.

He studied mathematics and physics and turned out to be a very bright young man who entertained and amused people with his brilliant experiments and observations. Galileo is our star, the people would say.

"It soon reached my ears that a certain Fleming had constructed a spyglass ... Upon hearing the news, I set myself to thinking about the problem ... Finally, sparing neither labor nor expense, I succeeded in constructing for myself so excellent an instrument that objects seen by means of it appeared nearly one thousand times larger and over thirty times closer than when regarded with our natural vision." (He and telescope was coined two years later, in 1611.)

Then one day Galileo heard about a new instrument for seeing things far, far away. He figured out how it worked and made one for himself. Then he turned it to the sky.

News of the telescope reaches Galileo

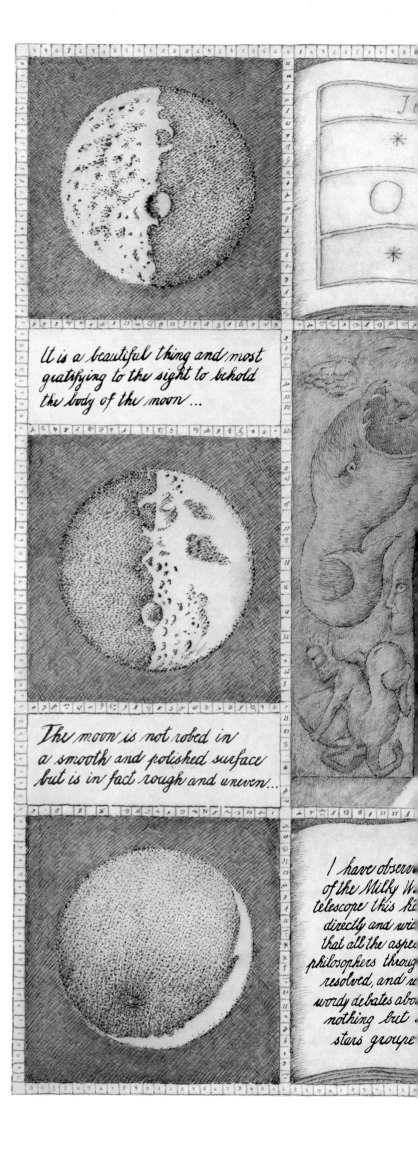

The Starry Messenger

Revealing great, unusual, and remarkable spectacles
opening these to the consideration of every man, and
especially of philosophers and astronomers;
as observed by Galileo Galilei
Gentleman of Florence
Professor of Mathematics in the
University of Padua
With the Aid of a
Spyglass
lately invented by him,
In the surface of the Moon, in innumerable
Fixed Stars, in Nebulae, and above all
in FOUR PLANETS
swiftly revolving about Jupiter at
differing distances and periods,
and known to no one before the
Author recently perceived them
and decided that they should
be named
THE MEDICEAN STARS

Venice
1610

It is a beautiful thing and most
gratifying to the sight to behold
the body of the moon ...

The moon is not robed in
a smooth and polished surface
but is in fact rough and uneven ...

I have observ...
of the Milky W...
telescope this ki...
directly and wri...
that all the aspe...
philosophers throug...
resolved, and...
wordy debates abo...
nothing but...
stars groupe...

Night after night, he gazed
through his telescope and wrote
down everything he observed.
Then he published his
observations in a book which
he called *The Starry Messenger*.

"(I) know-rather what sunspots are not than what they really are, it being much harder for me to discover the truth than to refute what is false."

"I have no doubt whatever that they are real objects and not mere appearances or illusions of the eye or of the lenses of the telescope."

"I liken the sunspots to clouds or smokes."

"I shall now describe the method of drawing the spots with complete accuracy... Direct the telescope upon the sun... Expose a flat white sheet of paper about a foot from the concave lens... With a pen one may mark out the spots in their right sizes, shapes, and positions."

Galileo was amazed by what he could see with his telescope.

MEDIC

SIDI

NV

MAGNA, LON

PHILOSOPH,

GALILE

Paiauni, G

QVATVOR

People read Galileo's book, and they became inspired. He made maps of the heavens and dedicated the four newly discovered "stars" of Jupiter to his patron and ruler, the Grand Duke of Tuscany, Cosimo II.

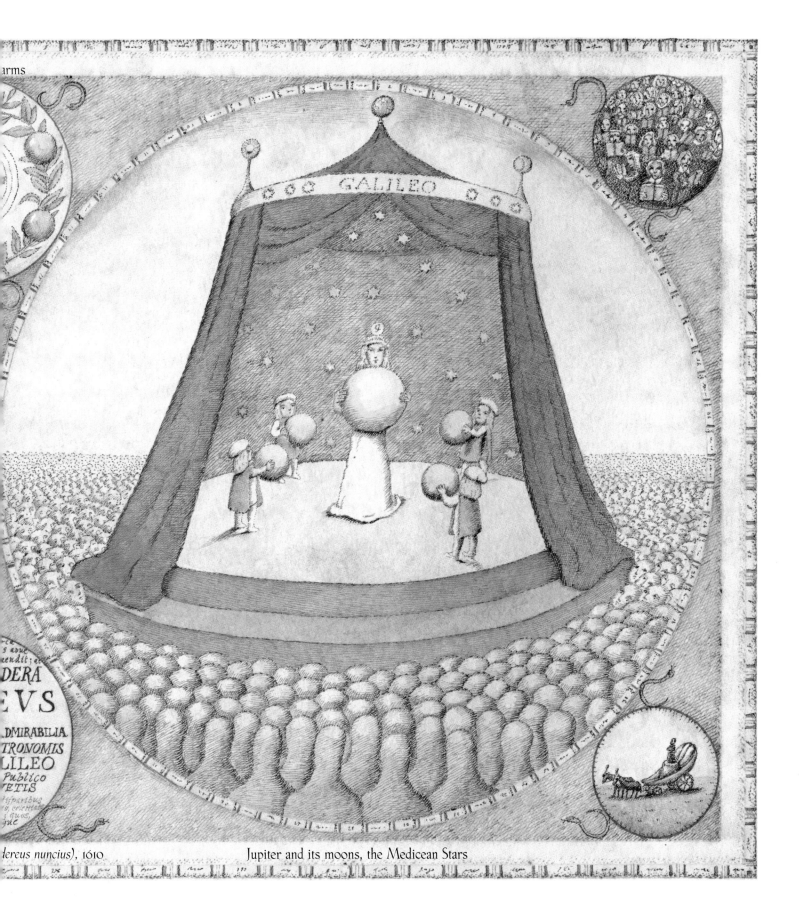

GALILEO

DERA
EVS
DMIRABILIA
TRONOMIS
LILEO
Publico
ETIS

lereus nuncius), 1610   Jupiter and its moons, the Medicean Stars

Gifts of a telescope and a copy of Galileo's book
were sent to all the kings and princes of Europe,
and Galileo was named Chief Philosopher
and Mathematician to the Medici court.

Hercules carrying the sky

Galileo's book was presented at the Frankfurt book fair *and was later translated into many languages, including Chinese.*

The Medicean Stars revolving about Jupiter

Soon Galileo was famous. More and more people celebrated the stars, and they celebrated Galileo and his discoveries with statues and parades and spectacular events.

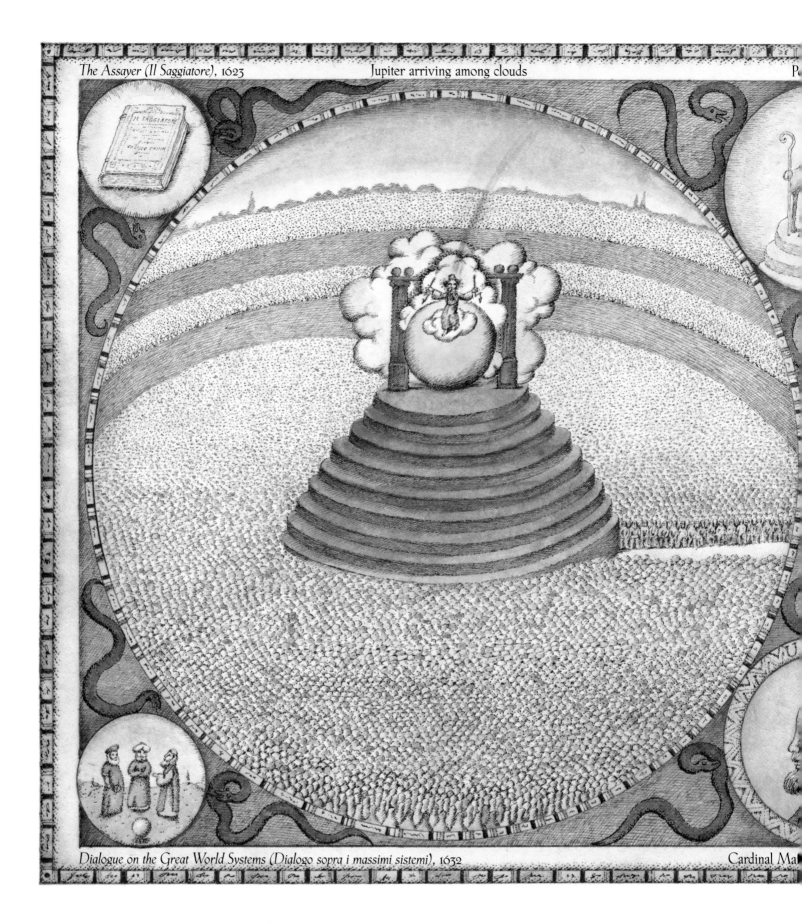

His fame grew . . . and the celebrations became extravaganzas.
But now the Church began to worry. Galileo had become too
popular. By upholding the idea that the earth was not the
center of the universe, he had gone against the Bible and
everything the ancient philosophers had taught.

"I hold the sun to be situated motionless in the center of the revolution of the celestial orbs while the earth rotates on its axis and revolves around the sun."

He had gone against the Church . . .

Galileo was ordered to stop believing what he could see with his own two eyes. He was summoned to appear before the highest ruler of the land—the Pope.

"I do not feel obliged to believe that the same God who has endowed us with senses, reason, and intellect has intended to forgo their use ... He would not require us to deny sense and reason in physical matters which are set before our eyes and minds by direct experience or necessary demonstrations."

"Why should I believe blindly and stupidly what I wish to believe, and subject the freedom of my intellect to someone else who is just as liable to error as I am?"

"....If they [the ancient philosophers] had seen what we see, they would have judged as we judge."

Galileo was afraid. He knew that people had suffered terrible torture and punishment for not following tradition. It could happen to him.

The Inquisition found Galileo guilty of heresy.

"Namely for having held and believed
a doctrine which is false and contrary
to the divine and Holy Scripture; that
the sun is the center of the world and
does not move from east to west, and
the earth moves and is not the center
of the world, and that one may hold
and defend as probable an opinion after
it has been declared and defined contrary
to the Holy Scripture"

June 1633 Rome

He was tried in the Pope's
court, and everyone could see
that the stars had left his eyes.

"In the sciences the authority of thousands of opinions is not worth as much as one tiny spark of reason in an individual man."

"With regard to matters requiring thought: the less people know and understand about them, the more positively they attempt to argue concerning them."

"I think that in discussion of physical problems we ought to begin not from the authority of scriptural passages, but from sense-experiences and necessary demonstrations (Nature)."

Galileo was condemned to spend the rest of his life locked in his house under guard. But he still had stars on his mind, and no one could keep him from thinking about the wonders of the skies and the mysteries of the universe. And even when he went blind, no one could keep him from passing his ideas along to others, until the day he died. But still the ideas lived on.

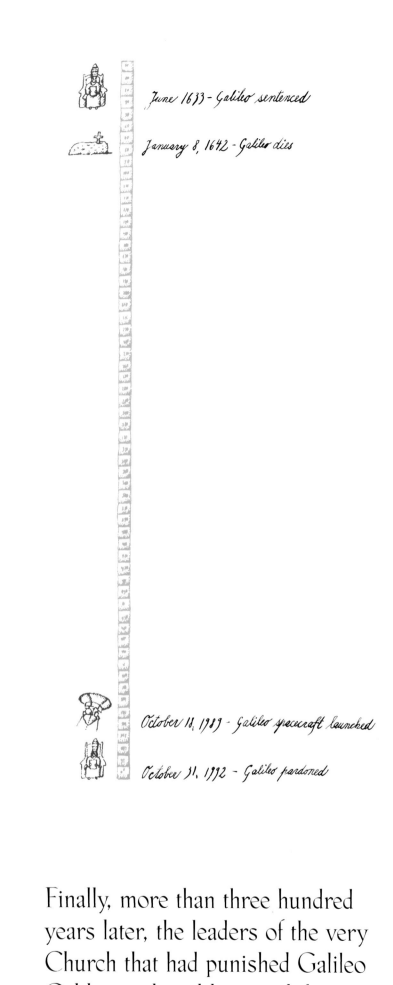

June 1633 - Galileo sentenced

January 8, 1642 - Galileo dies

October 18, 1989 - Galileo spacecraft launched

October 31, 1992 - Galileo pardoned

Finally, more than three hundred years later, the leaders of the very Church that had punished Galileo Galilei pardoned him, and they admitted that he was probably—in fact, surely and absolutely—right.

AFTER 350 YEARS, VATICAN
SAYS GALILEO WAS RIGHT